The Best Of
EAGLES
For Guitar

Includes SUPER-TAB Notation

Arranged by John Curtin

CONTENTS

LYIN' EYES

Words and Music by
DON HENLEY and GLENN FREY

Additional lyrics

2. Late at night a big old house gets lonely;
   I guess every form of refuge has its price.
   And it breaks her heart to think her love is only
   Given to a man with hands as cold as ice.

3. So she tells him she must go out for the evening
   To comfort an old friend who's feelin' down.
   But he knows where she's goin' as she's leavin';
   She is headed for the cheatin' side of town.
   (Chorus)

4. She gets up and pours herself a strong one
   And stares out at the stars up in the sky.
   Another night, it's gonna be a long one;
   She draws the shade and hangs her head to cry.

5. My, oh my, you sure know how to arrange things;
   You set it up so well, so carefully.
   Ain't if funny how your new life didn't change things;
   You're still the same old girl you used to be.
   (Chorus)

I Can't Tell You Why

Words and Music by
DON HENLEY, GLENN FREY
and TIMOTHY B. SCHMIT

Look at us, ba - by, up all night tear - in' our love a - part. Aren't we the same two peo - ple who lived through years in the dark? Oh, Ev - 'ry time I try to walk a - way,

'cause I love you.___ Noth - in' wrong as far as

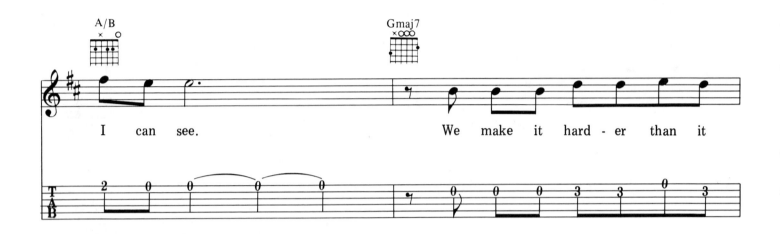

I can see. We make it hard - er than it

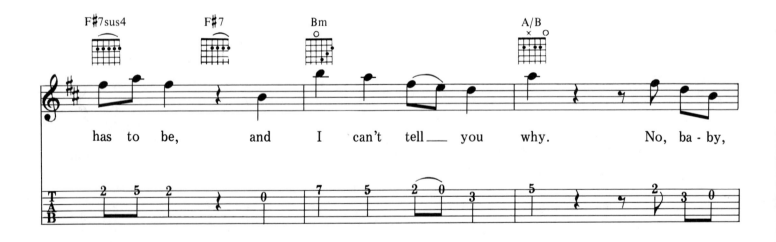

has to be, and I can't tell___ you why. No, ba - by,

I can't tell___ you why.___ I can't tell___ you

D.C. al Coda

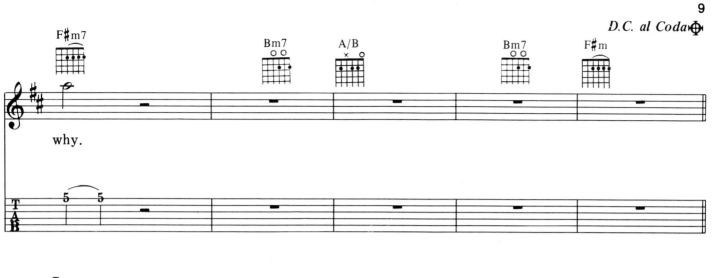

why.

Coda

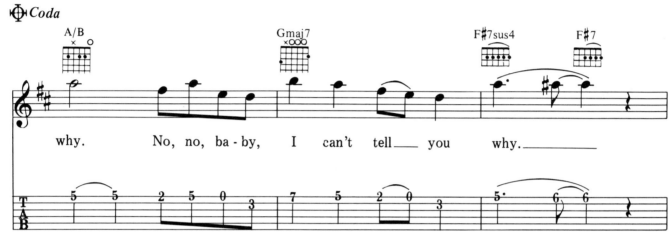

why.   No, no, ba - by,   I   can't   tell___ you   why._____

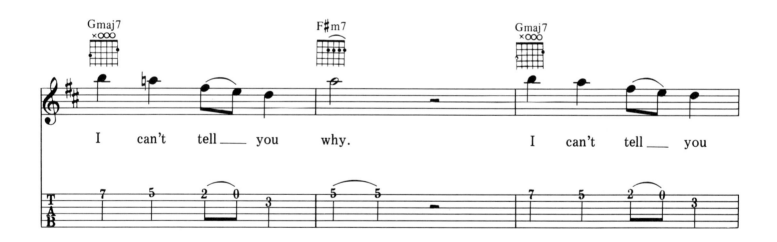

I   can't   tell___ you   why.   I   can't   tell ___ you

Repeat and fade

why.   *(Guitar)*

HOTEL CALIFORNIA

Words and Music by
DON FELDER, DON HENLEY
and GLENN FREY

Moderate Rock beat

On a dark des-ert high-way,   cool wind in my
Her mind is Tif-fa-ny twist-ed.   She got the Mer - ce - des

hair,   warm__ smell of co-li-tas __
bends.   She got a lot of pret-ty, pretty boys__

ris - ing up through the air. ____   Up a-head in the
that she calls   friends.__   How they dance in the

dis - tance,   I saw a shim-mer-ing   light.
court - yard;   sweet sum-mer   sweat.

Take It Easy

Words and Music by
JACKSON BROWNE and **GLENN FREY**

Additional lyrics

2. Well, I'm a-standin' on a corner in Winslow, Arizona, and such a fine sight to see,
   It's a girl, my Lord, in a flat-bed Ford slowin' down to take a look at me.
   Come on, baby, don't say maybe,
   I gotta know if your sweet love is gonna save me.
   We may lose and we may win, though we will never be here again,
   So open up, I'm climbin' in, so take it easy.

3. Well, I'm a-runnin' down the road tryin' to loosen my load, got a world of trouble on my mind,
   Lookin' for a lover who won't blow my cover, she's so hard to find.
   Take it easy, take it easy.
   Don't let the sound of your own wheels make you crazy.
   Come on baby, don't say maybe,
   I gotta know if your sweet love is gonna save me.

The Best Of My Love

Words and Music by
DON HENLEY, GLENN FREY
and JOHN DAVID SOUTHER

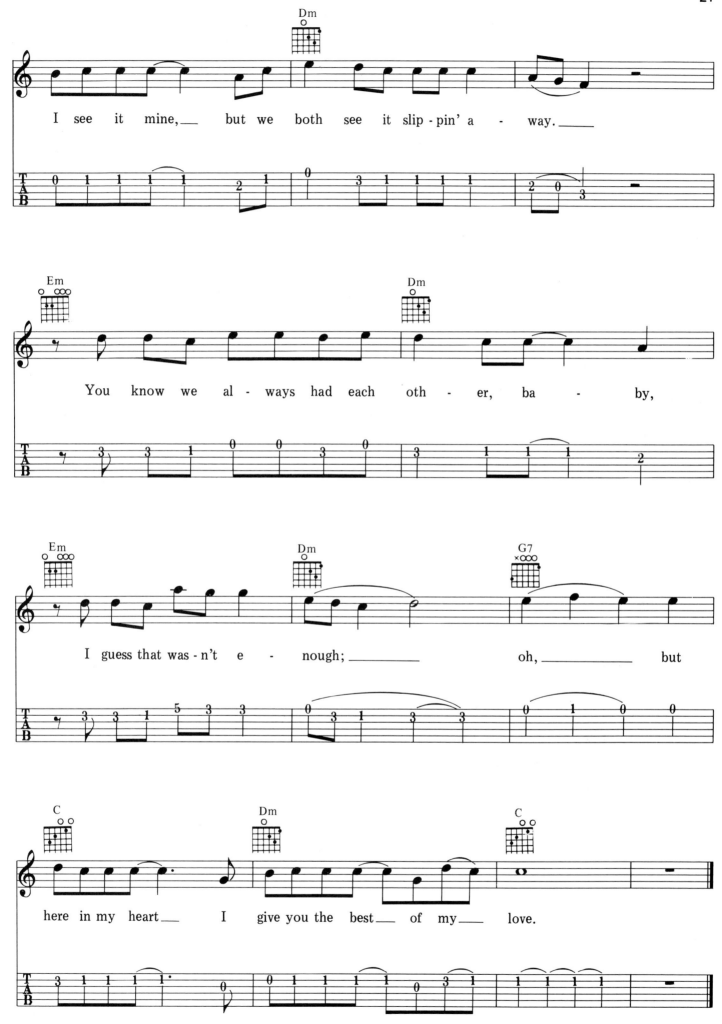

F/G
C
Dm
rough; I know you were try - in' to give me the best of your
bove; but here in my heart I give you the best of my
C
1.
G7
2.
G7
C
love.
love. Oh, sweet
Dm
dar - lin', you get the best of my love, oh,
C
Dm
sweet dar - lin', you get the best of my
Fm7
love. I'm go - in' back in time and it's a
T
A
B

Take It To The Limit

Words and Music by
RANDY MEISNER, DON HENLEY
and GLENN FREY

24

Witchy Woman

Words and Music by
BERNIE LEADON and DON HENLEY

Tequila Sunrise

Words and Music by
DON HENLEY and GLENN FREY

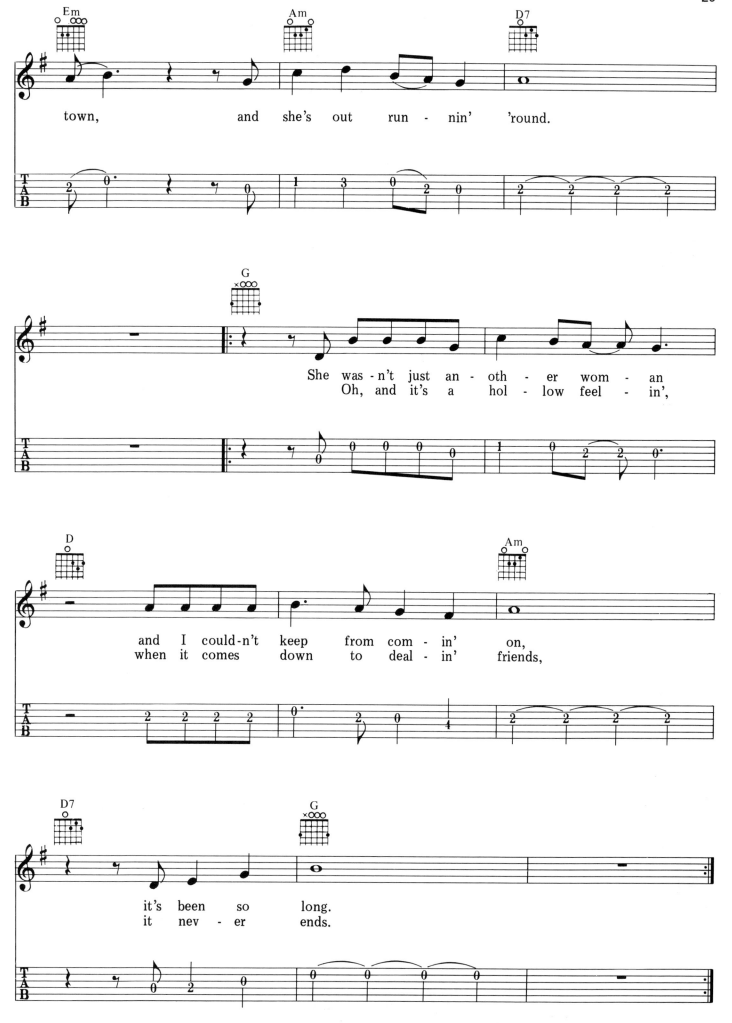

After The Thrill Is Gone

Words and Music by
DON HENLEY and GLENN FREY

Life In The Fast Lane

Words and Music by
JOE WALSH, DON HENLEY
and GLENN FREY

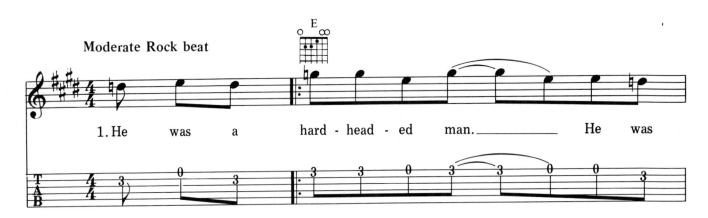

1. He was a hard-head-ed man._____ He was

bru-tal-ly hand-some, and she was ter-mi-nal-ly

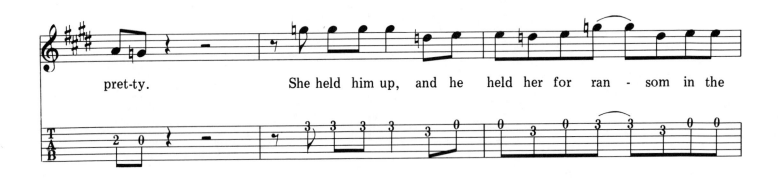

pret-ty. She held him up, and he held her for ran-som in the

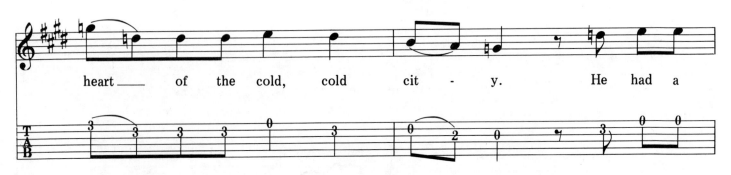

heart___ of the cold, cold cit-y. He had a

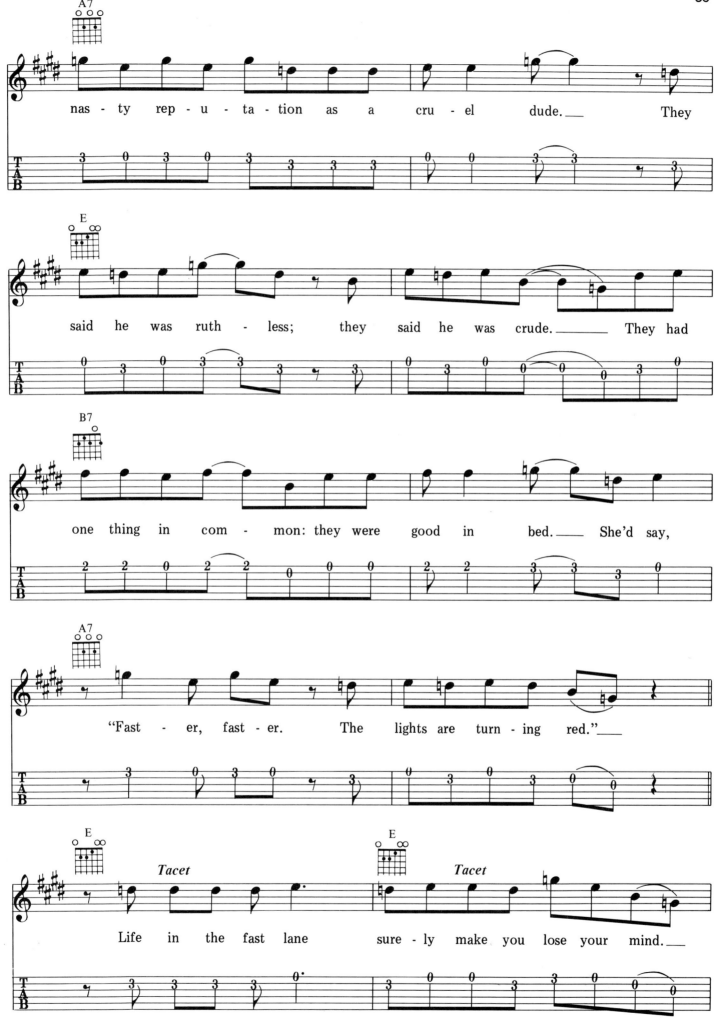

Life in the fast lane.

(Guitar)

Life in the fast lane; ev - 'ry - thing, all the time.

Life in the fast lane, uh huh. Life in the fast lane;

38

Additional lyrics

2. Eager for action and hot for the game,
   The coming attraction, the drop of a name.
   They knew all the right people; they took all the right pills.
   They threw outrageous parties; they paid heavily bills.
   There were lines on the mirror, lines on her face.
   She pretended not to notice; she was caught up in the race.
   Out every evenin' until it was light,
   He was too tired to make it; she was too tired to fight about it.
   Life in the fast lane *(etc.)*

3. Blowin' and burnin', blinded by thirst,
   They didn't see the stop sign; took a turn for the worst.
   She said, "Listen, baby. You can hear the engine ring.
   We've been up and down this highway; haven't seen a god-damn thing."
   He said, "Call the doctor. I think I'm gonna crash."
   "The doctor say he's comin', but you gotta pay him cash."
   They went rushin' down that freeway; messed around and got lost.
   They didn't know they were just dyin' to get off.
   And it was life in the fast lane *(etc.)*

ONE OF THESE NIGHTS

Words and Music by
DON HENLEY and GLENN FREY

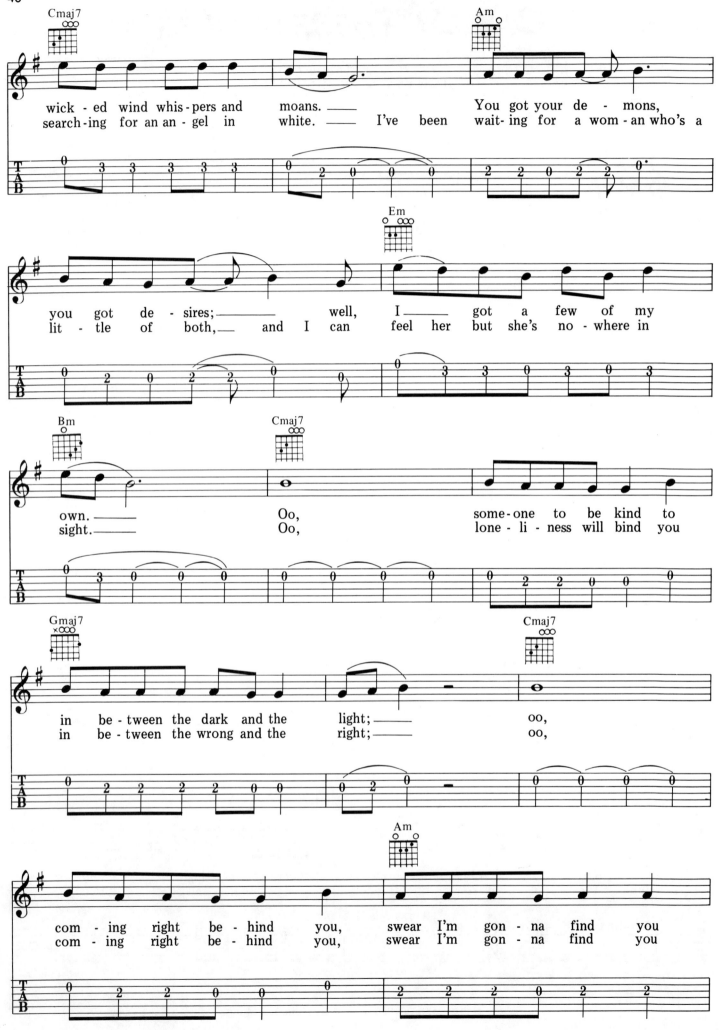

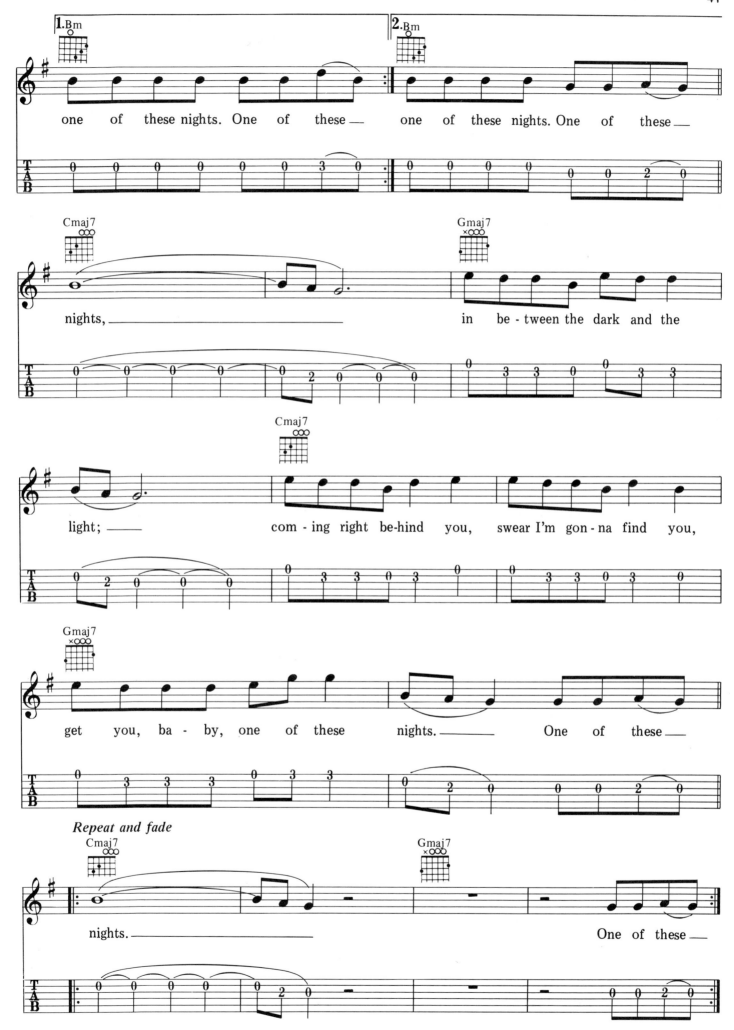

Heartache Tonight

Words and Music by
DON HENLEY, GLENN FREY, BOB SEGER
and J.D. SOUTHER

Moderate Blues beat

Some - bod-y's gon -na hurt some - one___ be-fore the night is through.___

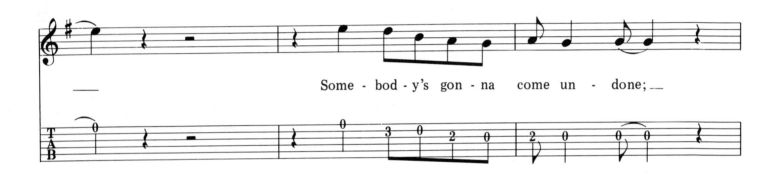

Some - bod - y's gon - na come un - done; ___

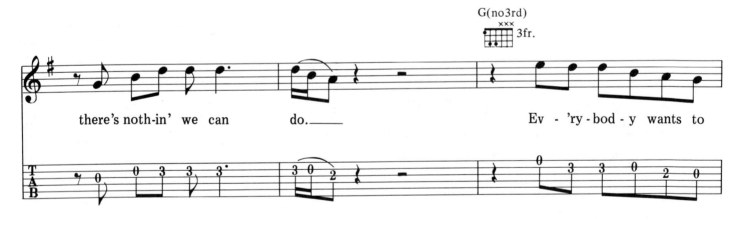

there's noth-in' we can do. ___ Ev - 'ry-bod - y wants to

touch some - bod - y, if it takes all night.

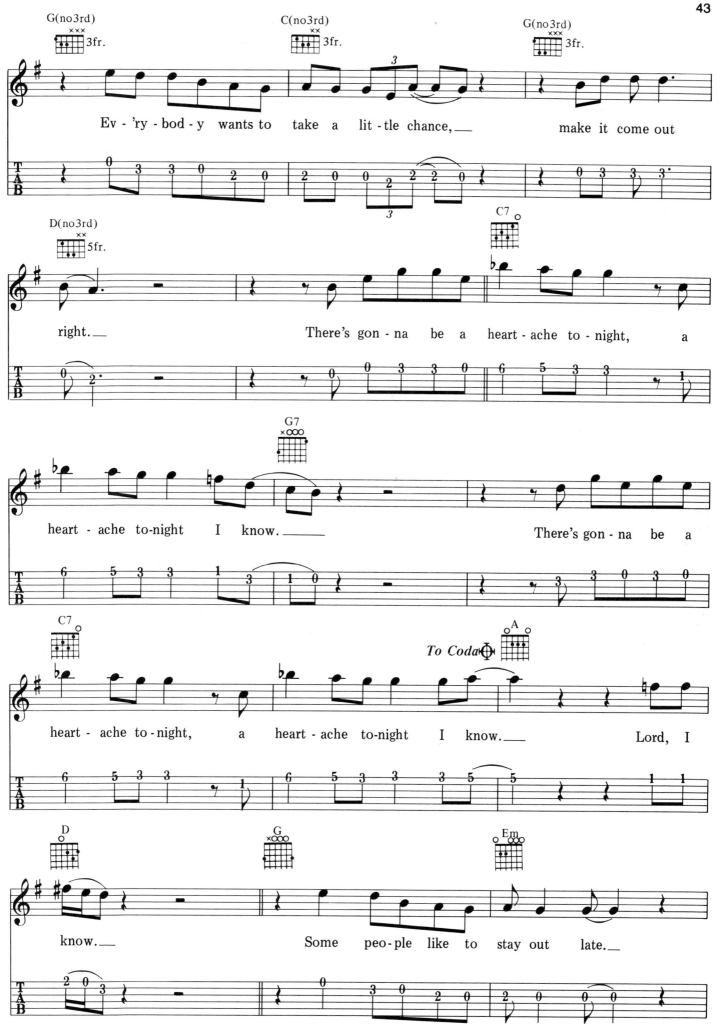

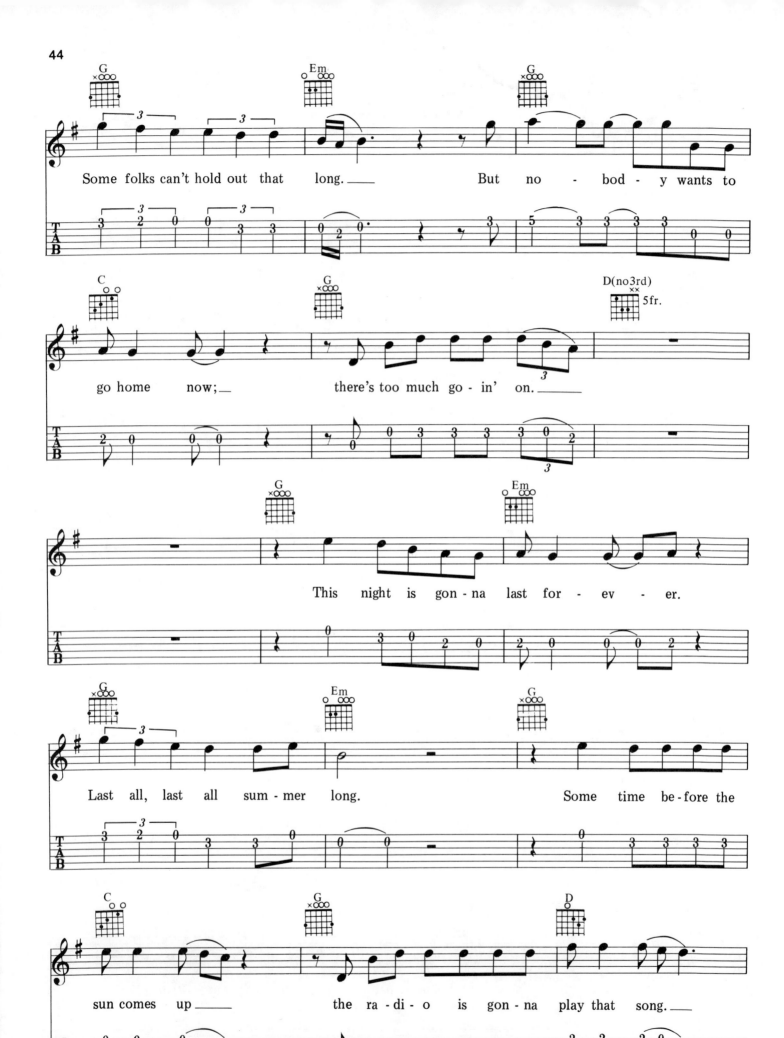

Some folks can't hold out that long. ___ But no - bod - y wants to

go home now; ___ there's too much go - in' on. ___

This night is gon - na last for - ev - er.

Last all, last all sum - mer long. Some time be - fore the

sun comes up ___ the ra - di - o is gon - na play that song. ___

heart - ache to - night, _____ a heart - ache to - night I know._

_____ Oh, I know._ There'll be a

heart - ache to - night, _____ a heart - ache to - night I know._

You Never Cry Like A Lover

Words and Music by
JOHN DAVID SOUTHER and DON HENLEY

Already Gone

Words and Music by
JACK TEMPCHIN and ROBB STRANDLUND

Additional lyrics

2. The letter that you wrote me made me stop and wonder why,
   But I guess you felt like you had to set things right.
   Just remember this, my girl, when you look up in the sky
   You can see the stars and still not see the light.
   (Chorus)

3. Well, I know it was'nt you who held me down;
   Heaven knows it wasn't you who set me free.
   So oftentimes it happens that we live our lives in chains
   And we never even know we have the key.
   (Chorus)

New Kid In Town

Words and Music by
JOHN DAVID SOUTHER, DON HENLEY
and GLENN FREY

Moderately

There's talk on the street; it sounds so fa - mil - iar.
You look in her eyes; the mu - sic be - gins to play.

Great ex - pec - ta - tions, ev - 'ry - bod - y's
Hope - less ro - man - tics, here we

watch - in' you.___ Peo - ple you
go a - gain.___ But af - ter a

meet, they all seem to know you.
while, you're look - in' the other way.

It's those

58

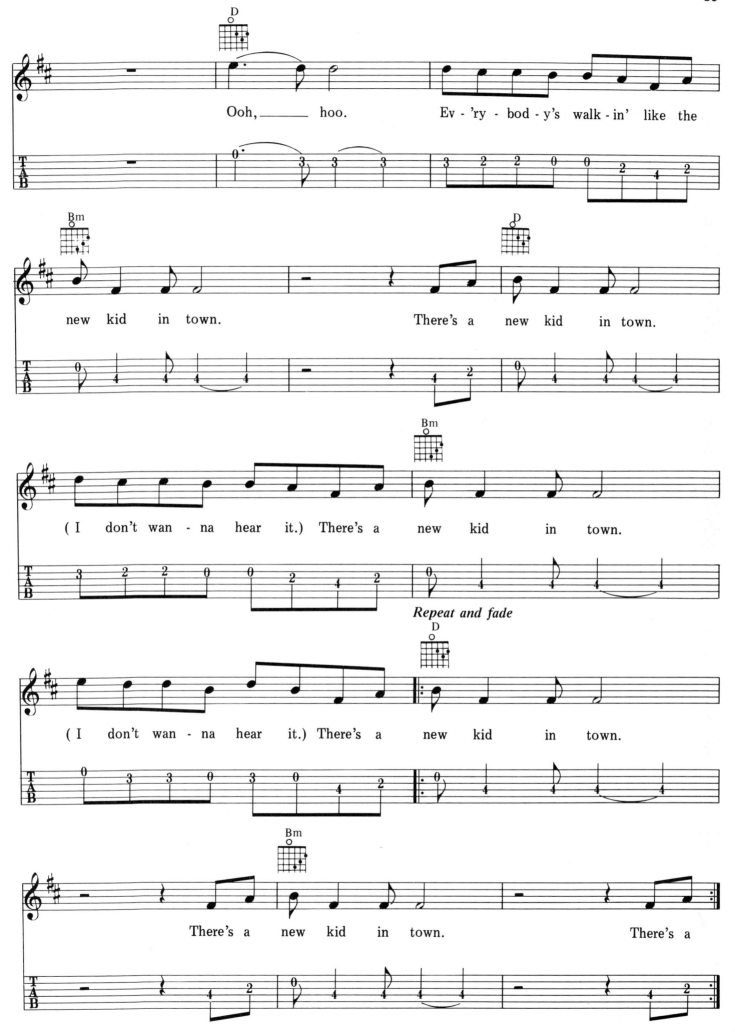

Peaceful Easy Feeling

Words and Music by
JACK TEMPCHIN

Moderate Country style

1. I like the way your spar-klin' ear - rings

lay a - gainst your skin so brown,

and I wan - na sleep with you in the

des - ert to - night with a bil - lion

Additional lyrics

2. And I found out a long time ago
    What a woman can do to your soul;
    Ah, but she can't take you anyway,
    You don't already know how to go.
    And I got a peaceful, easy feelin', *(etc.)*

3. I get the feelin' I may know you
    As a lover and a friend;
    But this voice keeps whisperin' in my other ear,
    Tells me I may never see you again.
    'Cause I got a peaceful, easy feelin', *(etc.)*

The Long Run

Words and Music by
DON HENLEY and GLENN FREY

Moderately

I used to hur - ry a lot; I used to
don't un - der - stand why you don't

wor - ry a lot, I used to stay out till the break of ___ day.
treat your-self bet - ter, do the cra - zy things that you do. 'Cause all the

Oh, that did - n't git it; it was high time I quit it, I just
deb - u - tantes in Hous - ton, ba - by,

could - n't car - ry on that ___ way. ___ Oh, I did some dam - age, I
could - n't hold a can - dle to you. ___ Did you do it for love? Did you

Desperado

Words and Music by
DON HENLEY and GLENN FREY